Owls

written by Anne Giulieri

An owl is a bird.
It is a bird
that lives *alone*.

Owls have:

head

ears

eyes

beak

wings

body

legs

talons

2

Owls have long *toes*
called *talons*.
The talons help
them to get *food*.

Owls do not have *teeth*.

Some owls are big
and some owls
are little.
This owl is tiny.
Look at the owl
and look
at the *pencil*.

This owl is very big.
Look at the *skateboard*.
This owl is long
like the skateboard.

The sun comes up
and owls go to sleep.

The sun goes down
and owls look
for food.
They can eat rats,
mice, frogs, *lizards*
and *snakes*.
They can also eat *worms*
and *insects*.

Owls have big round eyes to help them look for food in the *dark*.

Owls are called *nocturnal* animals.

Nocturnal animals eat and hunt at night-time.

Nocturnal animals sleep in the daytime.

Bats and foxes also eat and hunt at night.

We are not like owls.

We are not nocturnal.

We like to sleep at night-time,
and eat and play in the daytime.

Owls are very good
at hiding, too.
Can you see the owl?
It is hiding in the *snow*.

An owl is hiding in the trees.

It is brown and black.

This helps it to hide.

This is called *camouflage*.

Can you see the owl's food, too?

Hoot! Hoot!

Look in your garden at night-time.
Can you see some big round eyes?
Can you see an owl?

15

Picture Glossary

alone

insects

skateboard

teeth

camouflage

lizards

snakes

toes

dark

nocturnal

snow

worms

food

pencil

talons